ontents

Introduction

As you begin this five session study, it will be helpful for you to understand how the chapters are organized. First, the material has been written for adults, both lay and clergy, to be used for individual study or in small groups. The title for each chapter provides a key to understanding the correlation among the three lectionary readings: Old Testament, Epistle, and Gospel. A brief introduction at the beginning of each chapter develops the unifying theme for the Sunday's readings.

Each chapter is divided so that the three readings for the Sunday are listed with subtitles. The subtitles offer a key to that particular Scripture passage. At the beginning of the section that will interpret the Old Testament passage, for example, the reader will find motivational material designed to explore the significance of the text in advance of detailed study. Following this introduction, the reader will discover detailed information pertinent to understanding the text as it was intended to be understood by those who composed it. Then you will be invited to put into practice what you have read in Scripture.

Simply put, each Bible reading is presented in three phases: (1) explo-ration; (2) discovery; (3) applica-tion. Each subsection of each chapter follows this pattern. You will find numerous references to supporting Scripture passages throughout as well. The student who wishes to have an in-depth comprehension of the biblical message will benefit greatly from referring to these sup-plementary Bible passages.

As you begin your study, read each lection once for familiarity before reading the chapter. Keep your Bible open to the passage for easy reference. Have a notebook handy for making notes and for responding to questions or sugges-tions for reflection and action.

Underlying the chapters in this study is the broad theme, "The Coming King." As Christians preparing for the coming of the Lord Jesus Christ in this Advent sea-son, we know in advance that the king we are to expect is God's Anointed One, the Son of God. In order to appreciate the great significance of this announcement and to hear it as truly good news, it is important to explore the need for his coming.

Every generation of God's people has discovered the limits of its power to live well. If we want peace, we must work for justice. Our efforts, however, seem frustrating and impotent in the face of corruption, violence, greed, and disasters, which undermine our best efforts. The individual inclination to sin against God, self, and neighbor further strips the human family of its power to help itself. Repeatedly, faithful people have looked beyond themselves for salvation in a just and merciful God, sufficiently powerful to rescue them. God comes to us in the person of Jesus to establish God's kingdom on earth as it is in heaven. This is the good news we share.

The Day of the Lord Jesus Is Coming

Scriptures for Advent:
The First Sunday
Isaiah 64:1-9
1 Corinthians 1:3-9
Mark 13:24-37

The lectionary readings for the first Sunday focus on the readiness of the people of God to meet the Lord. Behind each of the three readings lies the primitive belief that no one can see God and live. No sinner can stand before God without being destroyed, for God is holy. Since no one is without sin, the day of the Lord's coming will be both great and terrible. It will be a day of judgment and condemnation in which humanity will be held accountable for its often tragic history and its pervasive unfaithfulness.

Each of the authors writes in the prophetic voice, calling the people to prepare themselves and reminding them that God is at work to purify them in preparation for the final judgment. The three writers expected God's coming to be soon. While the prophecy of Isaiah does not identify the coming One with a particular figure, the New Testament passages clearly indicate an expectation of the return of Jesus Christ.

GOD COMES FOR THOSE WHO WAIT FOR HIM
Isaiah 64:1-9

Surely the most crucial role anyone can play is that of parent. It is the parent's role to nurture, discipline, and release his or her children into independence. A parent's work involves profound intimacy as well as measured distancing at times, a watching from afar that encourages experimentation and affirms individuation.

One of the most difficult things a parent has to do repeatedly is to trust the child's judgment and skill, obedience and integrity, as well as strength of character and resilience when the child functions apart from the parent's watchful presence. For the child, the independence can be exhilarating and frightening, dangerous and opportune. Any parent who has ever sent a child to kindergarten or a teen to college knows the anxiety and the excitement of these transitional times. Waiting at home for the child's return can be harder than any other aspect of parenting. Yet, apart from this risk-taking, neither parent nor child can expect the fulfillment of an adult/adult relationship.

Still more difficult, however, is what popular psychologists call "tough love." Tough love requires children to suffer the consequences of their inappropriate, unwise, and unhealthy actions in order to recognize their errors and to begin the process of recovery and change. This stern discipline usually leaves parents feeling helpless and afraid, though justified. Children typically feel abandoned and at risk, while sometimes angry or ashamed. Yet, out of the tension and in the midst of crisis, character has the opportunity to form and new resolve can emerge.

Faith in self and in God may grow and, with them, a more mature parent/child relationship. A strong parent/child relationship, both in normal development over the lifespan and in times of extreme adversity, serves as an archetype of the dynamic interaction between creative beneficence and dependent vulnerability in the divine/human relationship.

The prophet Isaiah used this complex and vital archetypal relationship in describing the relationship between Judah and God: "Yet, O LORD, you are our Father; / we are the clay, and you are our potter; / we are all the work of your hand. / Do not be exceedingly angry, O LORD, / and do not remember iniquity forever" (Isaiah 64:8). Calling God "Father" to create the parent/child analogy for the divine/human relationship pointed in the direction of truth, limited as the language was by its anthropomorphism. The term *father* was rarely used for God by other authors of Hebrew Scripture; but it was, of course, used by Jesus when he taught his disciples to pray (Matthew 6:9).

Isaiah 64:1-9 is a prayer to God for mercy. The prophet represented the people of God before their Creator as before a parent who had deliberately distanced himself from his children in anger and for the sake of firm discipline (verse 5b). God had set the people free, and they had failed miserably. The people of Judah felt abandoned, as if they had been orphaned or, worse, betrayed in their trust toward their God (verse 7).

The people longed to see God again (verse 1). They wanted to know that God still lived and remained powerful to save and to help them. They remembered how God appeared to Moses as a flame in a bush to reveal the divine name and later appeared to give him the Law, leaving Moses' face glowing with the divine glory he had beheld. These events, divine epiphanies or self-revelations, defied rational explanation and astonished all those who heard of them, proving the reality and might of YHWH.

The prophet pleaded for a similar appearing on behalf of the people of God: "O that you would tear open the heavens and come down, / so that the mountains would quake at your presence— / as when fire kindles brushwood" (verses 1-2). The prophet and his people longed for reunion with their God, for they knew that with God's presence there would be joy and healing help.

As the prophet interceded for the people with God, he simultaneously reminded the people of the nature of God. God is a God of might who "works for those who wait for him" (verse 4). Isaiah remembered the past aloud and declared the greatness of the Lord above all other gods, seeking to lead his hearers into worship and active hope (verses 3-4). He knew that as the people turned toward their God, God would surely return to them (verse 5).

Verse 5 may present the most revealing and challenging spiritual insight of the entire passage: "But you were angry, and we sinned; / because you hid yourself we transgressed." Translators differ in their interpretation of the original Hebrew, but all serious interpreters of the text emphasize that the prophet and the people recognized their guilt. They knew that they deserved the suffering they experienced. They sensed that had God remained available and present for them, they may have repented and returned to lawfulness and faithfulness sooner.

Behind the argumentation and the obscurity of the language lies the truth that love heals best when it is present to touch and communicate. We call this love *grace.* It is undeserved and ever-present mercy, patience, long-suffering, and forgiveness that mitigates against anger, judgment, and unremitting grief. It is the faithfulness most familiar to us in the unconditional and enduring love of a parent toward his or her child. Still, it cannot be presumed upon. Isaiah confessed for the people their utter unworthiness of such grace.

The people had become like filthy rags fit only to rot—stinking and worthless—if not abhorrent to God (verse 6). No moral or spiritual character could be found among any of God's people. No one prayed or sought after God any longer (verse 7a). It seems that the people had lost all desire for salvation as a direct consequence of God's harsh action in abandoning the people to their sin (verse 7b). Nonetheless, the prophet dared to pray for the people, pleading with God to remember that God made Judah. All the people, even the worst of the sinners, belonged to God. Surely God would not turn away from Judah forever (verses 8b-9).

At the center of this unit of prophetic poetry lies the line, "You meet those who gladly do right, / those who remember you in your ways" (verse 5). This is the fulcrum on which the logic of this unit functions. The people wanted to experience God present with them. If they were going to know God intimately again, however, they would have to keep covenant with God. They would have to obey God's law and to return to the love of their Creator. In a sense, they would have to grow up and take responsibility for themselves and for a mature relationship with their God. Then the coming of the Lord would be more than mysterious fireworks. The Lord's coming would bring lasting peace and wholeness.

The wisdom of Isaiah's inspired message remains as true today as it was in 500 B.C. People still experience God as absent. They practice lifestyles that alienate them from the Source of their well-being and even from their own souls. They blame God or the church or religion instead of taking responsibility for their choices and behavior. Yet, the life-giving, life-transforming Spirit of God remains available to correct and to redeem the worst of us and the best of us. When we look up and out toward the One we most need, God meets us where we are and embraces us with the same gracious power that gave birth, life, and resurrection to the Lord Jesus.

How do you experience distance between yourself and God?

What can you do to turn toward God at this point in your life? How can you more actively await God's coming?

What can you expect from God as God's presence becomes real for you? How do you think God's being with you might change who you are and how you live each moment?

What does it mean for you that the same God who comes for you also comes for people you do not like, are afraid of, or do not know? Do you consider God "Father" only to other Christians? other people living in the United States? other persons of your race or ethnic background?

Might this Advent be a time of turning toward God with the wider community? How might such a possibility affect the way you keep this season holy?

THE FULLNESS OF GOD'S GRACE IS AT HAND
1 Corinthians 1:3-9

One of the most wonderful dimensions of the Advent season is the hospitality for which we prepare. Most of us will be guests in someone's home or will receive family and friends into our homes as a part of the celebration to come. In many cases these gatherings will be complex and interesting, if not challenging. Yet, they remain among the highlights of the year.

When I was a child living in Florida, my grandparents usually planned to travel south to be with us for Christmas. Their trip would be the beginning of their winter in the sunshine, snowbirds that they were in their retirement. When the day of their scheduled arrival came, I would go to the end of our street and stand or sit in active waiting, watching tirelessly for their car. When I saw it in the distance, I would smile, run, laugh, and cry all at the same time. They were the most precious people in the world to me, next to my parents, mostly because they counted me precious and were equally glad to see me. Today, I wait eagerly for the arrival of my adult children when the holidays come. Someday, I hope my grandchildren will look for my arrival as I did that of their great-great grandparents. This sense of eager waiting lies behind the spirit of Paul's letter to the church at Corinth.

Paul had seen the Lord by revelation. He was filled with a lively hope of seeing the Lord face to face. Paul expected Christ's soon coming and anticipated the grace and peace that the Lord's coming would bring. He believed himself called to prepare a people set apart and morally clean as a welcoming party. Paul had already worked hard to be sure that all was in order for the arrival of the One who is Lord and Savior.

Many signs of the Lord's coming were observable among the people. They were spiritually gifted. The prophecies of Jeremiah and Joel regarding the last days were being fulfilled in the Corinthian congregation in exceptional ways (Jeremiah 31:31; Joel 2:28-32).

Highly articulate, inspired, and insightful prophets, teachers, healers, ecstatics, and persons with gifts for administration, compassion, and acts of mercy were all present to extend the work of the gospel. These divinely empowered ministries indicated the close of the present age and served as a foretaste of the fullness to come.

Still, there was tension in the community; all was not well. Paul struggled with the concern that his work would be undone at Corinth if certain leaders failed to agree and if the immoral activity of which he had heard was not dealt with authoritatively and swiftly.

Paul addressed his beloved community as persons called to be saints (1 Corinthians 1:2). With the authority of one who had been with the Lord, he extended his pastoral embrace to all those who would read his letter. Paul spoke for God when he wrote, "Grace to you and peace from God our Father and the Lord Jesus Christ" (verse 3).

In using the words *grace* and *peace*, both of which were common in Greco-Roman and Hebrew greetings, Paul infused them with the fullness of meaning he had experienced personally and preached faithfully as an evangelist (Romans 5:1-2). This greeting was not merely a formality such as one would use in a business letter; it was a creative word from God given in order that the realities they described would become the current character of the Christian church at Corinth in the mid-fifties A.D. The letter to the Corinthian church was being written under divine authority.

As Paul proceeded to the introductory section of his letter, he built a bridge with his readers by expressing his profound gratitude to God, as if in prayer, for the goodness of God manifest among the people there (verse 4). As their founding pastor, he rejoiced in the validation of his ministry that was evident in God's gifting the people with the Holy Spirit and equipping them so thoroughly for supernatural ministries (verse 5). Theirs was a community of spiritual power. Paul found them to be rich in everything required for effectively strengthening the testimony of the Christian gospel in the region of Achaia, the southernmost district of Greece (verses 6-7).

Then Paul moved toward the matter of deepest concern to him as a mediator of the divine will and as an intercessor for the people. Verse 8 reads as a proclamation of his profound trust in the faithfulness of God to fulfill the saving covenant with "those who are sanctified" (verse 2). This apostle and pastor, one like unto Moses, prayed to God on behalf of the people even as he wrote to the congregation: "He will also strengthen you to the end, so that you may be blameless on the day of our Lord Jesus Christ. God is faithful; by him you were called into the fellowship of his Son, Jesus Christ our Lord" (1:8-9).

Paul believed that God was already present and active among the people of God at Corinth. Though Paul exercised his apostolic office at a distance in Ephesus, God was not far off. The Lord was at hand.

Paul envisioned a great homecoming in which the utter joy and peace of reunion with the Lord would be consummated (verse 9). He claimed, for his own benefit as well as for the sake of the people he served, the truth that God alone saves. The same God who sent the Lord Jesus Christ to purify the people in order that they might be worthy of the name, "the church of God that is in Corinth" (verse 2), would also preserve them blameless until the day of the Lord's appearing (verses 2, 8). Paul could relinquish ultimate responsibility for the preparedness of the people, though he had to press forward as an exhorter and pastoral overseer of the work.

As we, the people of God called to be saints in the twenty-first century, await the Advent or coming of the Lord in this season, we live in the in-between time with all the saints before us. While we have many and great preparations to make daily, even hourly, the fullness of the work is not ours to do. God is at work among us to cleanse, empower, encourage, forgive, and change us so that we will be more ready for him than we could ever imagine. The same Spirit of grace and peace that was in Jesus of Nazareth is at work and present among us already making preparations for the full disclosure yet to come. *Marana tha*—"Our Lord, come!" (1 Corinthians 16:22b).

If the founding pastor of your congregation or the current overseer of your region were to visit and evaluate the state of your church, what concerns would surface?

How might your faith community be found lacking in fitness to serve as Christ's emissaries in the world?

What behavior patterns would embarrass you?

Are you a party to any aspect of the unpreparedness?

What can you do to help get your community ready for excellence in holiness and in divine service?

THE SON OF MAN SHALL COME TO GATHER GOD'S PEOPLE FROM THROUGHOUT THE EARTH
Mark 13:24-37

In a global community in which all races mingle freely and a host of faith traditions influence daily conversation and behavior, the thought of a great day in which God will come to receive God's own seems thrilling and challenging. Surely that ingathering will include people we would not have expected. Most will be people whose languages we do not speak and whose faith practices are different from our own. So who will be among "the elect"? Will we be there, and how can we be sure?

A Muslim refugee family visited our congregation. Through one of the daughters, the mother asked me to visit in their home as soon as possible. Though I did so promptly with a sense of privilege and joy, I went with some fear as well. I knew that as an American representing Christ I might easily offend them, be misunderstood, or simply find it difficult to communicate meaningfully. I discovered that the head of the household, a United Nations relief worker and a professor in a major university in Afghanistan, had been murdered by the government of his country on the charge of being a Christian. He had been working for human rights, including medicine and education for women and girls. He had dared to associate with a Christian colleague and had paid the ultimate price. Now his family wanted to associate with me and with a Christian congregation in their new city while remaining faithful Muslims.

Their story and their courage moved me deeply. Soon I discovered that they had a high regard for Jesus and expected his return to judge the world and to defeat Satan. Much more important, I discovered within them a deep love for God, the One True and Living God. I will never be the same again for having met them. A lasting bond of friendship has developed between this family and the congregation they dared to visit. The exchange of understanding has broadened our view of God's people and led many of us into areas of ministry and service we had not previously envisioned, including working among Afghani refugees.

For the refugee family whose father and husband was martyred for his humanitarian work, a new sense of community has emerged. Among their friends are people whom they otherwise would have feared and shunned. Surely this family has experienced great persecution. They are also beginning to sense the salvation that is to come in the new and broader community of faith that has been formed as Muslims and Christians cry, pray, work, and break bread together.

Jewish, Christian, and Muslim people all look forward, through the writings of their prophets, to a day when God will vindicate the righteous, defeat the power of evil that presently controls the course of human history, and bring about a lasting peace. These world religions possess what scholars refer to as apocalyptic writings, which are based on divinely inspired visions. These texts describe what the faithful are to expect using vivid images and symbolic language.

All apocalypses, including Mark's, predict a great crisis in which cosmic accidents will signal a final conflict between Good and Evil, Light and Darkness, God and Satan. While some apocalyptic literature seems to inspire and to be motivated by a desire for revenge, however, Mark's apocalypse inspires hope and perseverance. The last days will be preceded by trouble and suffering but will lead to salvation for those who remain faithful to the end.

It is only natural for people who hear and believe such predictions to ask when these things will happen and how they will be able to recognize them when they occur. Mark's Gospel declares that the evidence of the Day of the Lord will be so universal that no one could miss it. The moment will capture everyone's attention at once. The coming of God's Anointed One will be as visible as are the sun and the moon. Nothing will be hidden. No special revelation or prophetic knowledge will be required.

Mark 13:24-27 foretells not only days of crisis among the celestial bodies but the coming of a divine representative in human form. First the sun, moon, and stars will cease to function normally, signaling the return of creation to its original chaos. Then the Son of Man will appear to bring order.

Who is the Son of Man figure of whom Mark's Gospel speaks? The term is one that the earliest record of Jesus' sayings places on the lips of Jesus as a self-designation. The term can refer simply to a human being. Jesus used it on occasion in place of the first person pronoun. It can also refer to God's emissary of final judgment, as described in the apocalyptic prophecy of Daniel 7:13-14. Jewish apocalyptic writing of the first century and earlier is known to have used the term as a title as well.

The apocalyptic Son of Man coming on the clouds of heaven is to be a man-like redeemer sent by God to accomplish the liberation of those who have lived according to God's will. Moreover, he will establish a lasting, international dominion and shall be its king forever. The first readers of Mark's apocalypse would have understood the implications of the phrase "Son of Man" and would have associated it with God's saving intervention.

If there will be no question about the time of his coming, how can we know that we will be among "the elect" he will come to vindicate? The elect are those whom the Son of Man judges to have endured great trouble and persecution in faithfulness toward God. The term does not imply predestination in the sense of an arbitrary selection process unknown to humankind. Rather, it refers to the will of God to save and to help all creation, linked with a response of obedience on the part of those who love and serve God. It is up to us to be among the elect or chosen people to be gathered from throughout the world.

Perhaps our thoughts in response to this powerful and strange set of images should reflect some healthy fear. With that may come some serious self-examination. Our expectations for peace may be tempered with a greater willingness to endure discomfort, danger, and self-sacrifice or to risk advocating for those who are suffering oppression, particularly religious persecution. Perhaps out of this year's Advent season will be born a new open-mindedness, a more serious respect for the faith and experience of those different from ourselves, and fresh insight into the way we should prepare for the coming of the Lord Jesus Christ.

What might you eliminate from your traditional Christmas preparations in order to find time and energy for a more faithful and thoughtful expression of your readiness for the coming of the Lord?

What trouble and suffering might you be avoiding now but are being called to accept as an act of faithfulness?

Do you know anyone who is currently burdened or hurting while serving humanity and doing the work of God in the world? How might you work with him or her as an act of faithfulness to God?

Prepare the Way of the Lord

Scriptures for Advent: The Second Sunday
Isaiah 40:1-11
2 Peter 3:8-15a
Mark 1:1-8

Underlying the lectionary readings for the Second Sunday of Advent is the experience of wilderness. Anyone who has traveled to contemporary Israel through the Jordan River Valley knows the desert that served the prophets and poets of Israel as an ever-ready metaphor for desolation. Mer-chants and pilgrims forced to journey that way in ancient times faced the dangers of wild animals, thirst, and heat exhaustion, as well as thieves assaulting them at night from the shadows of the mountains.

Thoughts of being in the desert inspired fear. At the same time, however, people seeking refuge from the hectic pace of urban life in Jerusalem or from the moral and spiritual corruption of the more densely settled cities and farming communities would retreat to the wilderness for prayer and fasting, alone or in a monastic community. There they could be still and silent long enough to hear the pure, refreshing voice of God.

While the wilderness could mean death, it could also bring new vision and fresh faith. Although the desert is a specific geographical place that can be visited, it functions as a metaphor within and without the passages under study. As a symbol, the wilderness suggests and invites us to something more.

THE WAY OF THE LORD
Isaiah 40:1-11

One of the most enduring elements of the season of Advent is its fine art. Whether we hear Handel's *Messiah* performed or behold the beauty of a stained glass window depicting the Annunciation, we find ourselves invited by the genius and faith of the inspired artist into a dimension of truth that defies notation or imagery. Sounds, colors, forms, sacred story, poetry and ritual acts all help to create a pathway from where we are to where God is.

The beauty of the composition, the excellence of the language, and the exalted vision of the prophet make Isaiah the Hebrew Scripture most consistently read by Christian congregations around the world in every generation, not only during Advent but year-round. When studying this particular text, we examine fine art. Much more, however, we experience a "highway for our God" (Isaiah 40:3). If we seek to understand not only with our minds but with our souls, this prophetic poem can lead us to the Lord.

Scholars call this unit of the larger poem an oracle of consolation. It announces the imminent restoration of Judah. In order to enter fully into the imagery of the poem, however, it will be useful to explore several components that are implied but not explained.

First, the prophet understood himself to be present to overhear a discussion in the throne room of the King of the universe. He heard God commanding a messenger to declare a time of comfort for Judah. The prophet believed himself to be that messenger (verses 1-2).

Second, God, the King, has many heavenly servants. These angelic beings act as a cabinet might with a president (1 Kings 22:19-22). Isaiah overheard their interaction (Isaiah 40:3, 6, 9).

Third, the wilderness or desert symbolizes the suffering that the people of Judah had endured for some time at the hand of God who had judged them and condemned their unfaithfulness. It recalls the forty-year wandering during which the first generation of Hebrews who escaped from slavery in Egypt all died but out of which a new generation emerged to enter and conquer the Promised Land. The wilderness also recalls the exile of the citizens of Judah to Babylonia, by way of a long journey through a desert wasteland after the Temple and the land of Judah were despoiled. It represents chaos and danger. Most important, however, the wilderness suggests that God will transform it into a pathway of safety, freedom, and restoration for the people of God on their way home to rest and peace.

Fourth, the poem envisions God as a great and triumphant warrior king returning from battle against Judah's enemies. The heavenly king journeys with his entourage toward Zion and all of Judah with the good news of having defeated the adversary. He enters to liberate the land. He does not come with the usual spoils of war but brings with him the people of God, as a shepherd leading his sheep to safety. The exiled and desolate people return to reclaim their heritage over a highway built for their God.

Verses 1-2 form the first stanza of the oracle. God speaks. The message is simple. The people have paid in full for their sin. As thieves caught in their deed must pay back twice the value of what they stole, so Judah had "received from the

LORD's hand double for all her sins" (Isaiah 40:2; Exodus 22:7). The debt was paid in full. The prisoners would be released.

Isaiah 40:3-5 forms the second stanza of the unit. One of the heavenly servants in the divine council chambers "cries out" (verse 3). He speaks as a herald with a loud voice. The announcement functions as a creative act, an order that must be implemented. It is divinely authorized (verse 5). The great divide between exile and home, with all its obstacles, must be transformed into a road fit for a king (verse 3). Valleys will be filled and mountains leveled (verse 4). The royal company traveling on it will be visible from one end of the highway to the other. In fact, it will attract international attention simultaneously: "All people shall see it together" (verse 5).

The third stanza, verses 6-11, includes a dialogue between one of God's heavenly servants and the prophet (verses 6-8). Isaiah is commissioned to announce the vast difference between God and humanity and between the decrees of the people and the Word of God. People are transient like grass. They grow old and die. They become dust as God wills it. Their word fails. God, on the other hand, is everlasting. God's Word, once spoken, remains true and effectual. By implication, God's promised consolation can be trusted.

Verses 9-11 seem to be addressed to the congregation. God commissioned the people to become prophets. They were to watch for the fulfillment of the promised consolation. Metaphorically, they were to climb the tallest mountain so as to be able to see at a distance the coming of the Lord (verse 9). When they saw their king's entourage on the horizon, they were to make the announcement so that all could hear and celebrate the news in advance (verse 9). They were to report the reassuring word that God, the King, had gained victory.

God would compensate the nation for its long-suffering and desolation (verse 10). God who had dealt harshly with the people would exercise great care and mercy toward them. God would use great power to nurture and sustain the people as a shepherd cares for the mother sheep and their young (verse 11).

Is God speaking to us in this passage? Like all art extracted from its original context and apart from the interpretation of the original artist, this great prophetic poem must be translated into terms we can hear for our time, if it is to serve us well. Perhaps this oracle belongs to the poor and oppressed of the earth and not to us after all (Luke 6:20-26). Yet deep at the core of our experience is a sense of spiritual hunger and moral disease. Life has become complex beyond anyone's anticipation (Matthew 5:3-5). Violence, corruption, and disease devastate the global community in spite of enhanced technology and intervention on the part of peacemakers from many nations.

The majority of the world's citizens live in poverty and hunger, without adequate medical care or personal safety, while North Americans consume a disproportionate amount of the food, medicine, and fuel used annually. Our moral debt to the majority of the world's people and to future generations is vast. Meanwhile, we and all the first-world nations lack the will and, in a very real sense, the power to resolve the problems within and beyond our borders.

Have we any right to expect com-fort and consolation in our time? Have we really paid our penalty? Probably the answer, according to any form of justice we know, is a resounding no. However, justice is being superseded by God's mercy. By divine decree, the comfort belongs to us, not because of who we are, but because of who God is. After all, we cannot seem to resolve our own problems. Nothing, however, is impossible with God.

We must cease our self-examination and listen for the encouragement that requires nothing of us but hope and faith. It is not we who must build an interstate through the wilderness of the world's problems. Rather, God does what only God can do. Just as the author of the Gospel of John portrayed the Baptist calling from the wilderness, "Here is the Lamb of God who takes away the sin of the world"

(John 1:29), so we recognize Jesus as the highway of our God, the way of the Lord, the means by which God comes to save and to help us in our spiritual, moral, and societal destitution.

The wilderness of the twenty-first century shall become the dwelling place of God in the Spirit. The church must dare to become a herald of good news, announcing peace and grace.

How is your church preaching morality and announcing the presence of a redeeming God?

How is your church seeking to create the kingdom of God on earth or daring to trust that God will build it with or without us? How do you experience the tension between these two points of view this Advent?

Where do you perceive evidence of the coming of the Lord to your area?

How might you help others to see and to prepare the way for what God is doing?

GOD'S TIME AND OUR TIME
2 Peter 3:8-15a

Everyone who lives long enough experiences major disappointment and the struggle to recover from the loss involved. Perhaps a marriage has left you disillusioned. Maybe parenting a particular child has left you with guilt, fear, and a sense of inadequacy. Possibly a vocational choice has proved mistaken or an employer has proved unreliable. In all of these and myriad other similar circumstances, disappointment forces us to reassess our beliefs, values, choices, and direction.

In the midst of such uncertainty we are vulnerable to discouragement and loss of hope. Poor advice or shallow relationships can betray us. Drained, we can fall into behavior patterns that, ultimately, defeat our best intentions and undermine our sense of integrity. The consequences can be truly punishing.

On the other hand, disappointment and disillusionment can also lead to necessary personal growth. When old ways of relating to others or to the universe become dysfunctional, the crisis we experience can be the catalyst for searching, finding, and entering a new way of being that is far more fulfilling and appropriate. In a sense, we will have wandered in a wilderness, desolate and lost, but emerged humbled, simplified, and clear about what matters. The disillusionment, our desert time, will have prepared us for a new and better day.

The congregations to which Second Peter is addressed were in the throes of a debate and some confusion regarding the failed expectations for the coming of the Lord within the lifetimes of the first apostles. The early church anticipated an imminent resolution of the injustices of history, including the defeat of Satan and the judgment of the unrighteous, by no later than A.D. 90. They expected the way of the Lord to be built through their century's wilderness experience; yet they had outlived their sense of God's timing. Now they were lost in a different kind of moral, spiritual, and theological wilderness.

Jesus, according to the apocalyptic tradition preserved in the Synoptic Gospels, predicted that the generation alive at the time of his ministry would see the kingdom of God established. Matthew quotes Jesus: "Truly I tell you, there are some standing here who will not taste death before they see the Son of Man coming in his kingdom" (Matthew 16:28; see also 24:34; Mark 9:1; Luke 21:32).

First-century Jewish apocalyptic prophets and rabbis, as well, promoted the widespread expectation that the Messiah would soon come. Both Christians and Jews believed that the Messiah's coming would lead to a new heaven and a new earth in that the righteous would be vindicated and God's will would be done. A great deal of hope was, therefore, focused on this event and on the moral preparation required.

The letters of Paul indicate a similar sense of timing. In the early A.D. 50's, Paul wrote, "For the Lord himself, with a cry of command, with the archangel's call and with the sound of God's trumpet, will descend from heaven, and the dead in Christ will rise first. Then we who are alive, who are left, will be caught up in the clouds together with them to meet the

Lord in the air; and so we will be with the Lord forever" (1 Thessalonians 4:16-17).

Paul expected to be living and active in ministry, along with many of his converts, at the time of the coming of the Lord. He was motivated to seek the Word of the Lord on the subject, however, because already at mid-century some were perplexed about the apparent delay. Some of the believers had died without seeing the fulfillment of the apocalyptic expectations that had been so widely embraced (Matthew 5:17-18; 24:34-35; Mark 13:30-31; Luke 21:32-33).

The author of Second Peter, writing near the turn of the century and long after most had expected the Day of Judgment and the coming of the Lord, was dealing with increasing disillusionment with the gospel as it had been presented. The disenchanted believers were searching for explanations and listening to anyone who might offer some new and more satisfactory doctrine. False apostles, claiming to speak for the Lord, taught that the judgment would not occur after all and that the immutable universe would remain intact. No calamity such as the fire of judgment could destroy the course of things, they insisted. Even more serious, they taught by their example that the moral rectitude implied in the soon coming of the Lord was unnecessary.

Ethical laxity was setting in among the Christian churches.

A crisis was emerging. This was a season of theological transition, spiritual malaise, and moral confusion. The author wrote as a pastoral encourager and a defender of the apostolic faith, basing his argument on Hebrew Scripture.

In attempting to rescue his congregations from heresy and moral decay, the author proposed that God's timing was different from ours (2 Peter 3:8; see also Psalm 90:4). Moreover, what seemed to his readers to be a delay was, in fact, evidence of God's great mercy and patience toward those who had not yet repented of their sin (2 Peter 3:9; see also Joel 2:12-14; Amos 5:18-20; Jonah 4:2). The writer alluded to Jesus' teaching regarding the surprise that would occur for the unprepared upon the coming of the Son of Man, as if a thief suddenly broke in during the night (Matthew 24:36-44; Luke 12:39-40).

Having advanced these proposals, the writer asserted that the cosmos would return to its original chaos through fire at the time of judgment. On that day the deeds and thoughts of the entire human race would be "disclosed" or found out, thus reasserting the moral implications of his doctrine and Jesus' repeated call to remain awake (2 Peter 3:10; Matthew 24:42; 25:13; Mark 13:35-37; Luke 12:40).

The author and the spirituality by which the congregation was formed taught that personal righteousness or holiness indicated readiness for the coming of the Lord and that such preparedness would actually hasten his much longed for arrival (2 Peter 3:11-12, 14). This inner readiness included sincere repentance relative to past behavior and a consistent, daily discipline of living according to God's law and holding one's self accountable in Christian community.

Christians were to be "without spot or blemish" at the time of the coming of Christ, as attested widely in Christian literature (Ephesians 1:4; 5:27; Philippians 1:10; 2:15; Colossians 1:21-22; 1 Thessalonians 3:13; 5:23; Jude 24). This moral purity and preparedness implied a profound relationship of faith in Christ and an abiding hope of his return to consummate God's saving work (2 Peter 3:15a; Matthew 19:28; Romans 8:18-21). Clearly, by implication, the false teachers were not pursuers of peace and were unprepared. They would be found out on the Day of Judgment and be destroyed.

The apocalyptic worldview that the writer assumed and that his adversaries brought into question was a worldview that he had adopted from Jewish apocalyptic as well as from the broader base of Hebrew Scripture (Deuteronomy 32:22; Isaiah 66:15-16; Zephaniah 1:18). Jews had always believed that God intervenes in history for the purpose of saving God's people and punishing the wicked. Hellenizing Jews and Christians, influenced by such philosophical movements as Epicureanism, proposed that God does not, after all, intervene or judge. These alternative views may well have been part of the problem that led to the crisis the author addressed.

A significant feature of the apocalyptic vision described by cross-cultural literature of the period was a fiery end of history. Fire was an ancient symbol of God's presence, as well as of God's judgment, among Hebrew peoples. Note the vision of the burning bush that Moses saw and out of which he received his call. Remember the pillar of fire that led the Hebrew people in the wilderness at night. Remember also the fiery destruction of Sodom and Gomorrah. Isaiah 34:4 suggests that the stars, the sun, and the moon will all decay at the close of history; the elements of the cosmos will be destroyed. Thus, fire as a feature of the Judgment Day suggested an ultimate coming of God to return creation to its original fiery origin. Out of this furnace would emerge a new creation.

The author, holding the hope of the soon coming of the Lord and of a new creation dear, articulated his vision brilliantly when he wrote, "We wait for new heavens and a new earth, where righteousness is at home" (2 Peter 3:13). The troubled congregations to whom he wrote would one day live beyond confusion and doubt, as well as beyond the reach of heretical teachers and undermining doctrine. They would rest in the joy and peace of the glorious company of the Lord and all the saints.

The author's defense of the apostolic hope and his urgent call for moral rectitude was only one early act of leadership on the long journey toward readjusting the expectations of the church and preparing the way for the coming of the Lord. Other spiritual leaders would offer further assistance and interpretation, for the clarion call to remain alert morally and spiritually, preserving a deep expectation of the Lord's coming, remains clear and true over nineteen centuries later.

How has your scientific education informed your concept of the universe and forced you to think differently from our first-century predecessors?

How does God intervene in history generally? How have you experienced God's breaking into your life?

Can you conceive of the close of history? What do you think will happen? Do you expect God to be in control of the final events? Do you expect to see Christ?

How will the judgment of God take place? What do you need to do now in order to be confident of your place among the people of God now and forever? How will you prepare for the coming of the Lord?

THE SPIRIT-BAPTIZER AND THE WATER-BAPTIZER
Mark 1:1-8

A young couple, both of whom were raised in Christian churches and Christian homes, stumbled over a recent attempt to articulate their understanding of the gospel. It became clear that the term was so familiar that it had become vague, inviting highly subjective interpretation. While both had begun to respond personally to the good news of their faith traditions, they knew that they needed to learn more in order to clarify their understanding.

The first phrase of Mark 1:1 introduces the term *gospel* or "good news": "The beginning of the good news of Jesus Christ, the Son of God." The "good news" refers to the essential message of the early Christian movement. It does not refer, as some might think, to the literary genre (gospel) that the writer had chosen or to the preaching of Jesus of Nazareth. Neither does it refer, as the young couple thought, to the personal faith of those who identify themselves as Christians, though many Christians embrace the teaching of the apostles, precisely as the first Christians carefully passed it down from one generation to the next.

The "good news" that first-century Christians preached and taught was the simple message that Jesus of Nazareth is the *Christ*, the *Son of God*. Those titles have become almost as familiar to Christians as the word *gospel* is ambiguous in its meaning. Mark's use of the terms invites careful study.

The title *Christ*, while it has become something like Jesus' surname in common Christian usage, originally identified Jesus as the Jewish Messiah. The word *Christ* is simply the Greek form of the Hebrew word *messiah*. The Hebrew word for *messiah* may be translated literally as Anointed One (1 Samuel 10:1).

Mark, and all early Christians with him, believed Jesus to be God's chosen instrument of salvation and the one whom the great Hebrew prophets had foreseen. According to early Christian preaching, Jesus fulfilled the promises of God to save and to help God's people. Jesus' coming signaled the beginning of a great age of holiness and harmony with God. The Messiah was greater than any king before him, though each of the kings of Israel and Judah had been greeted by their subjects as God's Chosen or Anointed One. Jesus Christ would reign forever; and his dominion would perfect justice, mercy, and peace for all creation.

The term *Son of God*, while closely related to the word *messiah*, is derived from a distinct tradition. In this context, it refers to the ongoing hope that the king would love the will of God and do it and that an ideal king would emerge to fulfill that hope and to bring God's redemptive work to fulfillment. He would act so as to enforce God's law, such that God's will would be done on earth as it is done in the heavenly domain, thus demonstrating his moral and spiritual kingship with God.

A Hebrew king was adopted by God as a son of God upon his anointing and coronation: "I will tell of the decree of the LORD: / He said to me, 'You are my son; / today I have begotten you'" (Psalm 2:7; see also Psalm 89:26-27). Furthermore, the term *Son of God*, when applied either to the king or to his subjects, points to the belief that all are dependent on God as their Father for their existence, viability, and power and that God will care for them as does a father, both in provision and in discipline (2 Samuel 7:13-16).

Mark's preferred title for Jesus surfaces again at the Crucifixion when the centurion, a pagan, declares, "Truly this man was God's Son!" (Mark 15:39). Both *Christ* and *Son of God* express the confidence of the early Christian community as they reflected on the identity of Jesus.

John the Baptist's role was simply to prepare the way for the coming of the Messiah. He was not the Messiah and was much inferior to him, but his work was necessary. Mark quotes from Isaiah 40:3 and Malachi 3:1 in 1:2-3. John's work was to function as an advance messenger, preparing the way and warning the people of the coming of the Messiah, lest his coming bring condemnation rather than blessing (Mark 1:4). They were to turn away from their former disobedience and to be restored to inner purity by the forgiveness of sins, as symbolized by washing themselves in water.

John's work took place in the wilderness to the east of the Jordan River where the great heroes of Israel before him—Moses, Elijah, and David—had spent time in prayer and encountered the Lord. It was here also that the people had crossed the Jordan upon entering Canaan under Joshua's leadership. The wilderness was the place where men of God went to purify themselves and to commune with God. Qumran, a desert retreat for the Essenes, an ascetic community that practiced ritual bathing, was located near the site where John baptized with water. Mark saw in the setting of John's ministry a symbolic verification of his work as following in the great tradition of the Hebrew prophets. John the Baptist accomplished the work of Elijah in preparing the way of the Lord (Malachi 4:5).

While water baptism indicated the readiness of the people to receive the Messiah with joy, water baptism merely made the people ready for something much greater: Spirit baptism. Water baptism was effectual for the moment. Spirit baptism radically altered the relationship of the recipient with God and ensured lasting holiness.

John's ministry and his anticipation of Jesus' ministry had been foretold by prophets before him: "I will sprinkle clean water upon you, and you shall be clean from all your uncleannesses, and from all your idols I will cleanse you. A new heart I will give you, and a new spirit I will put within you; and I will remove from your body the heart of stone and give you a heart of flesh. I will put my spirit within you, and make you follow my statutes and be careful to observe my ordinances" (Ezekiel 36:25-27; see also Jeremiah 31:31-34).

The Essenes likewise believed that the sons of light, faithful members of their community who expected in their lifetime a final conflict between God and Satan, would be given the Spirit of the true counsel of God. John may have associated with the Essenes and been influenced by them, but he carried on a separate apocalyptic ministry, believing that the Messiah was to appear imminently in the person of a faithful Jew whom God had chosen. This one, so much greater than himself that he would not be worthy even to serve as his slave, would have the power to provide a moral and spiritually transforming ministry the effectiveness of which would be permanent (Mark 1:7-8).

The gospel of Jesus Christ, the Son of God is, therefore, good news that the time of Spirit baptism has come. God is pouring out the refreshing, renewing, restorative power of his Spirit on all who reorient their lives toward God through faith in God's Anointed One. Jesus comes to replace the sinful hearts of the people with new hearts that love God and are inwardly motivated to fulfill God's will. They will live in peace with God and with one another under the controlling influence of God's Spirit. The kingdom of God is arriving! Are you prepared?

The Prophets Testify to the Coming One

Scriptures for Advent:
The Third Sunday
Isaiah 61:1-4, 8-11
1 Thessalonians 5:16-24
John 1:6-8, 19-28

Human beings long to hear from God, whether consciously or unconsciously. All people seek knowledge and foresight that is otherwise unavailable to them as a way of preparing themselves to meet the unknown. Most of us recognize how limited our wisdom is, how short our vision is, how fallible our expectations are, and how fruitless our long-term planning often is due to our inability to foresee all that will occur. We want to enter the future with caution and savvy, hence the increasingly widespread turning to psychics in the absence of true prophets who can speak for God.

From ancient times in all the cultures of the Near East, prophets were charismatic figures with unique powers of insight and speech. They were understood as speaking directly for the gods or the highest of the pantheon of gods. Canaanite prophets, active when the wandering Hebrews entered the Promised Land, would fall into ecstatic trances and utter oracles in unintelligible languages. Similar bands of prophets lived together around holy places and wandered among the Hebrews. Every generation had its seers. Often they were supported by the king and hired to support his political and military pursuits.

The great Hebrew prophets were distinct, however, from the men and women who experienced intermittent ecstasy, uttering unintelligible sounds. These prophets experienced the Spirit as remaining with them and making them profoundly articulate. Some of the finest literature of the Hebrew Scriptures can be found in the form of messages from the prophets Isaiah, Jeremiah, Hosea, and Amos.

The prophets' communion with God was so intimate that they developed a divine pathos, a sympathy with God and an ability to speak with divine authority. They sat in the throne room of God and heard God's counsel directly by way of visions, dreams, and prayer.

Afterward, they spoke for God to the people. Sometimes they interceded for the people with God; but more often they called the people to return to God in repentance and in obedience.

Frequently, in times of trouble, these men of God offered words of hope, promising God's deliverance from their enemies. For a period of three to four hundred years, however, no great prophet arose among the Jews. As a result, in companionship with apocalyptic expectations, popular faith expected the return of the prophetic voice as a sign of the end of the age and the coming of the Day of the Lord.

John the Baptist followed in the footsteps of great prophets such as Elijah and Isaiah. His coming signaled, for many, the final days leading to the long-awaited salvation of God. The Spirit of the Lord was with him, and he attracted crowds of people from all classes and parties (Matthew 3:7; Mark 1:5). John, like the prophets before him, called for repentance and lives "worthy of repentance" (Matthew 3:8).

From early in his ministry, Jesus was understood as a prophet, though some recognized him to be more than a prophet. He spoke "as one having authority, and not as the scribes" (Mark 1:22). Following Jesus' ministry, death, and resurrection, the Spirit of prophecy was given to the church; and Christian prophets exercised their ministries wherever communities of faith organized.

Early Christian prophets continued their ministries over the course of many years, much as did apostles, evangelists, pastors, and teachers. They were recognized as called, gifted, and appointed by God to fulfill their particular service as mouthpieces for the risen Lord, speaking the oracles of God to the church in the name of Jesus (Act 11:27; 13:1; 15:32; 19:6; 21:9-10; 1 Corinthians 12:28-29). Evidence of their work can be found particularly in the Gospel of John, with its long speeches and unique sayings of Jesus unparalleled in the Synoptic Gospels.

Christians approach the need to anticipate the future and to hear from God differently than do those who consult psychics or horoscopes. We trust that the essential truth we need to know has already been given in the life and ministry of Jesus. In him we find wisdom and grace sufficient to meet any challenge according to the will of God. In this sense we acknowledge him to be the very Word and Wisdom of God.

We know that we must submit our anxiety about the future to God in prayer. We believe that God is mysteriously and wonderfully at work within us and in the world to bring about order, meaning, and purposeful living. We know that it is as we open ourselves to the Spirit of Christ that the truth will become an integral part of our lives. We will not need to turn to persons with unusual powers for divining in order to find guidance.

The Spirit of God has been spread abroad and given to all the faithful. God's Word may come to us through one of the members of our church, while singing a hymn, or in the stillness of prayer. Our responsibility, then, is to become ever more true to the faith of Jesus and to watch and wait for God's Word.

AN EVERLASTING COVENANT
Isaiah 61:1-4, 8-11

Behind the oracle of Chapter 61 lies an earlier message found in Isaiah 59:21: "And as for me, this is my covenant with them, says the LORD: my spirit that is upon you, and my words that I have put in your mouth, shall not depart out of your mouth, or out of the mouths of your children, or out of the mouths of your children's children, says the LORD, from now on and forever."

The writer of this part of the Book of Isaiah understood himself to be the heir of this covenant. He was a descendant in the spirit of Isaiah, as were the people Judah, all of whom were called to be servants of God. The spirit of prophecy was present and active among the covenant people.

Usually the charismatic prophet, while uttering an oracle, was translated into an altered state of consciousness and was no longer functioning rationally. He or she did not control the message being uttered as a scribe at his desk might do. The prophet, likewise, did not control the boundaries within which the utterance was to be interpreted. Rather, the Spirit of God speaks for all who hear and interprets the Word for their time and setting.

Each generation must receive the covenant and its message as its own. John the Baptist may have drawn on this and similar oracles when he predicted that one mightier than himself would "baptize . . . with the Holy Spirit" (Mark 1:8). Likewise Jesus, according to Luke 4:16-27, identified himself with the speaker and quoted this passage when interpreting himself to his hometown. It is his reference to Isaiah 61 that makes the passage exceedingly important to the Christian tradition.

This unit of the longer poem can be divided into five sections. In verses 1-3, the prophet speaks of himself as being anointed. As he does so, he surely remembers the anointing of Saul and of David by the prophet Samuel. Likely he recalls the last words of King David recorded in 2 Samuel 23: "The spirit of the LORD speaks through me, / his word is upon my tongue. / The God of Israel has spoken, / the Rock of Israel has said to me: / One who rules over people justly, / ruling in the fear of God, / is like the light of morning, / like the sun rising on a cloudless morning, / gleaming from the rain on the grassy land" (verses 2-4).

The connection between anointing with the Spirit and anointing with oil is ancient and implied in the identity and work of the prophet in this oracle, as is the connection between the prophet as a servant of God and as a ruler in Judah. He feels himself clothed in the Spirit of God. A power from beyond himself has possessed him and equipped him to preach, to heal, and to liberate. He has become God's man, a servant of God for his time.

The prophet's work is to give an oracle of salvation for the righteous remnant of God's people. He will announce an eschatological event signaling the culmination of history. He will do more than preach encouragement, however; for this is the very word of God. The work of God shall be to reverse current conditions among the people so that those in poverty, those who mourn the state of the nation, and those oppressed by their overlords will find themselves rejoicing in the blessings of salvation.

The people whose courage and stamina have been drained and whose determination to follow God's law has been sorely tested will be "called oaks of righteousness" (Isaiah 61:3b). They will prove the power and majesty of their God by their living. All the people of God will experience themselves clothed with garments fit for the ultimate celebration, the salvation they have longed for. A headdress or garland and a mantle or tunic of praise will be their vestments for the Day of the Lord. It will be as if they are attending a marriage feast for the people Judah.

The second section, verses 4-5, shows the people strengthened to restore their habitation. The ruined cities and farms will be rebuilt and will become prosperous. The economy will flourish, and foreigners will work the fields as hired laborers. Poverty will be no more.

The lectionary omits the third section, verses 6-7, and moves to the last two. The fourth section is verses 8-9. Key to understanding these verses is the clause, "I will make an everlasting covenant with them" (verse 8b). The section revolves around that promise. It reflects the promise found in Isaiah 54:10: "My steadfast love shall not depart from you, / and my covenant of peace shall not be removed, / says the LORD, who has compassion on you."

The people had been burdened by the corruption of their overlords. There was no justice and no relief from oppression. God determined to rescue them and to compensate them. Instead of poverty and injustice, the people would enjoy fame and peace. They would be known as blessed by their God (61:9b).

The final section (verses 10-11) describes the anticipatory ecstasy of the prophet who was privileged to foresee the festal joy of salvation. His ecstasy took him into the future and allowed him to celebrate all that God would do for the people. It is as if the prophet danced inwardly in his garments, his robes, his garlands, and his jewels. He was filled with praise and delight in sharing the glory of God. He believed that all he saw in advance would surely be accomplished, just as a garden produces plants from the seeds that are sown in it. All the world would see the blessing of God in Zion (verse 11).

At this time of year there are many parties and concerts. Have you thought about what you will wear to the next occasion? The question sounds vain and frivolous unless asked in the context of this passage. The tradition of buying new clothes or wearing lush velvet at this time of the year may seem like self-indulgence unfitting good stewards. Isaiah did not see it that way, nor did the people of Judah. When they celebrated, they did so with all their senses.

Check your wardrobe. Do you have something special that you might wear meaningfully this year as a sign of your joy in God, a testimony to your belief in the coming One?

Do you know someone who has little to wear and nothing fitting for a celebration? Buy or make something for him or her, and share the meaning of the tradition that you have freshly discovered in this study of Isaiah 61.

KEPT BLAMELESS AT THE COMING OF THE LORD
1 Thessalonians 5:16-24

The first letter of Paul to the Thessalonians provides valuable insight into the development of Christianity and the Gentile mission in Europe. Thessalonica was located in the Roman Province of Macedonia in the northernmost part of Greece on the seacoast. The congregation there was Gentile or non-Jewish. They had been converted from paganism by Paul's gospel, having found in his message a superior God and a higher morality. This God was approachable and reliable. This God called for a quality of life more excellent than anything they had seen resulting from the various cults of the Greco-Roman world.

By converting, however, the Thessalonians had alienated themselves from their community. Gone were the economic and social opportunities and advantages they had enjoyed previously. Even their personal safety was at risk apparently. They were experiencing the costs of being Christian. Moreover, they were anxious about their loved ones who had died and what this might mean for them as they awaited the soon coming of the Lord (1 Thessalonians 4:13-18). Paul wrote to them as an overseer of their souls and of the mission he had established.

Already Paul had reminded the Thessalonians of their moral responsibilities, particularly within the community of faith. The church was to model the reign of God in their midst. Their behavior would serve to draw others in. The peace they enjoyed in their fellowship would sustain them through troubled times if they kept their focus on the Lord's coming.

It was out of this context, then, that Paul admonished them to "rejoice always" (5:16). He was not asking them to be happy about their circumstances. Rather, he insisted that they worship often, reminding themselves of the blessings of God's Spirit in their midst and anticipating the redemption that would surely come. Joy, rather than anxiety and doubt, was to characterize their daily living and to testify to their faith in the coming One.

Likewise, they were to "pray without ceasing" (verse 17). By praying continually, they would be putting their needs and their gratitude before God, honoring God with their thankfulness for all that they had already received and all that was yet to come. In prayer and celebrative worship the Thessalonians would find themselves communing with God's Spirit. Their spirits would be refreshed and their community renewed for courageously meeting opposition.

Paul felt it necessary to assert that what he required of them in these spiritual disciplines was not merely his own good advice but the very will of God (verse 18b). He believed that an active spiritual life was essential to their endurance and faithfulness. God had given them the means of remaining without blemish at his coming to judge the world. Those means included prayerful thanksgiving and joyful anticipation of the Lord's coming.

The church at Thessalonica, like all the congregations Paul founded, was rich with spiritual gifts. They were a Spirit-empowered community. Unfortunately, not all manifestations of the Spirit were authentically from the Lord. False teachers had arisen among the Thessalonians, claiming to speak for Christ while undermining Paul's reputation and message. Jesus had warned that such men would masquerade as genuine prophets, leading the vulnerable astray (Mark 13:21-22).

Impure motives and trickery had apparently infiltrated the church and called all manifestations of the Spirit into question (1 Thessalonians 2:3-4). Paul knew that to repress the movement of the Spirit was to cut off the life-flow of the church. Still, the believers would need to exercise caution and discernment in listening for the Word of God from any of the prophets.

Every word of prophecy had to be evaluated on the basis of the gospel that they had received originally from Paul (5:21a). Every message had to be considered for its purity and goodness, lest it beguile the hearers (verse 21b). The true prophet would testify that Jesus is Lord and call the church to rejoice in serving him: "You know that when you were pagans, you were enticed and led astray to idols that could not speak. Therefore I want you to understand that no one speaking by the Spirit of God ever says 'Let Jesus be cursed!' and no one can say 'Jesus is Lord' except by the Holy Spirit" (1 Corinthians 12:2-3).

Paul's final word of instruction summarized all that he had previously written regarding the godly life the Thessalonians were to lead (1 Thessalonians 4:2-7). Paul exhorted his readers to "abstain from every form of evil" (5:22). His goal was for the church to be morally and spiritually clean, prepared to meet the Lord. Paul was eager to present the church to the Lord as the fruit of his life's labor: "May your spirit and soul and body be kept sound and blameless at the coming of our Lord Jesus Christ" (verse 23b; see also 3:5b, 13).

Paul had worked hard in the past and had labored prayerfully in the Spirit as he composed this letter of encouragement and exhortation. He was convinced that God was speaking to the church through him (4:8). Nevertheless, in the end, the sanctification of the church and its salvation were God's work. Paul had to yield control and ultimate responsibility to God: "May the God of peace himself sanctify you entirely. . . . The one who calls you is faithful, and he will do this" (5:23a, 24).

The sanctification or purifying of the soul, spirit, and body of which Paul speaks is something he believed God's Word and Holy Spirit accomplish. Paul expected a transformation of the entire self and of the church, in anticipation of the new life that will be revealed in the resurrection of the dead (Romans 6:17-23).

Paul's sense of calling to the work of announcing the gospel of our Lord Jesus Christ inspired his belief that all were being called by God to the faith of Jesus. The call of God was as urgent and definite in the life of the local Christian who lived out his or her faith as an artisan or a homemaker as it was in the life of an itinerant apostle. God calls all of us to prepare to meet the Lord who is soon coming, according to the gospel Paul preached. All are called to be brothers and sisters to one another by faith, spiritual kin in the midst of family division and opposition, faithful to the end.

The work, however, is beyond human strength. Paul said, "The one who calls you is faithful, and he will do this" (1 Thessalonians 5:24). The goodness of Paul's prophetic and pastoral voice had been proved according to the standard he established. From beginning to end he testified, "Jesus is Lord," assured of his coming soon to complete the work already underway.

What might you do to rejoice in the Lord this week? Perhaps it is time to go caroling with others from your church, taking joy to shut-ins or to the elderly or to people living in a group home or a nursing home. Maybe you have a recording of worship music just waiting to be played. Perhaps it is time to write a card or a letter to someone who is not on your usual mailing list. Tell them about a holy moment in your life, and remind them of God's presence with them.

Are you burdened with something in your life or concerned

about someone else? Are you grieving the loss of someone you love? Spend time in prayer until your faith is restored and you rest assured in God.

Are you confused by some aspect of your faith that no longer makes sense to you? Pray for discernment. Wait and listen deeply. Know that God is at work in you to purify your mind and innermost self as you seek the truth.

THE WORD MADE FLESH
John 1:6-8, 19-28

Often we approach Advent and Christmas thinking only of the birth of Jesus and the events surrounding his birth, based on an homogenized narrative derived from all four Gospels. A lectionary study, however, invites us to think critically and to approach the message of this season with a more informed faith.

Each of the Gospel writers introduced the Christian message differently. Mark offered no account of the origins of Jesus—his birth, his parents, or his childhood. From Mark's perspective, the story began with the ministry of John the Baptist and Jesus' anointing as God's beloved Son upon his baptism in the Jordan River. In John's Gospel, however, the Christian message begins before the time of the Creation. The Word is presented as pre-existing all that is, and through him creation comes into being. The public ministry of Jesus, according to John's Gospel, begins with the witness of the prophet John the Baptist to the identity of the man Jesus (John 1:6-8). According to John's Gospel, the Baptist was neither a prophet of judgment nor one who called the people to repent. His function was to prepare the way for the coming of the Lord by pointing him out to the crowds.

John did not foretell events that would take place in the future, as some hope prophets or diviners will. Instead, he proclaimed the truth about Jesus. He served, above all, as a witness. He saw and knew who Jesus was by way of the Spirit who dwelt within him, giving him prophetic insight and prophetic utterance.

In the Gospels of Mark, Matthew, and Luke, the writers link Malachi 3:1 and Isaiah 40:3 with John the Baptist in identifying his role. Note that in John's Gospel, John the Baptist interprets himself. He quotes the prophecy: "I am the voice of one crying out in the wilderness, / 'Make straight the way of the Lord' " (1:23).

John took authority to bear witness to Jesus on the basis of that Scripture, which defined his call and his commission from God. The slight difference of approach follows out of this Gospel writer's emphasis on belief in Jesus as the key to eternal life. The reader can enter with confidence into life and light on the basis of the Baptist's testimony, as well as on the basis of the many other signs and witnesses to

Jesus to be recorded in the remainder of the Gospel.

When John's Gospel refers to Jesus as the light in verses 6-8, the author introduces one of many key word images that point to the revelation of God in and through Jesus. Jesus' life is a divine epiphany. God is made known in the person of the man Jesus. All the transcendent glory of the Lord is present in him. Moreover, his ministry will enlighten darkened souls and reveal the truth to those who believe, as light shining in a dark space reveals facts that otherwise could not be known with any clarity. All this is the gift of God to the world, freely available to all who will receive it.

As God spoke creation into existence in the beginning, making light before making anything else that was made, so the Word of God has brought about a dramatically new and good element of creation in Jesus, the Light of the world (Genesis 1:3).

During the first century, both before and after the ministry of Jesus, a cult of John the Baptist existed separate from the Essenes and the disciples of Jesus. For the purpose of clarifying the distinction between John the Baptist and his movement and Jesus and his followers, John's Gospel reports a dialogue (John 1:19-28).

Jewish inquisitors asked John the Baptist on what authority he carried out his work, basing their questions on assumptions typical of current apocalyptic expectations. The Essenes, and probably the Pharisees as well, expected either the prophet Moses or the prophet Elijah, neither of whose burial places had been found and both of whom were believed to have been taken up into heaven, to return before the coming of the Messiah to prepare his way (Deuteronomy 34:6; 2 Kings 2:11; Malachi 4:5). Since John testified that he was neither of these prophets but, instead, the prophet described by Isaiah 40:3, his adversaries doubted his right to baptize.

According to John's Gospel, John the Baptist redirected the attention of the inquisitors from an examination of his credentials to the ministry of the One whom he preceded. In this manner, the writer also redirects the reader's attention. John the Baptist is important only as a transitional figure and is not to be followed. Eternal life comes through faith in Jesus Christ.

What do you think of Jesus? Who is he to you? Why do you study his life and work?

If you experience God through him, what is the nature of the God you see revealed in him?

The Son of God Comes to Bring About the Obedience of Faith

Scriptures for Advent:
The Fourth Sunday
2 Samuel 7:1-11, 16
Romans 16:25-27
Luke 1:26-38

A friend of mine was raised in a strict, Christian household. Until his mid-teens, he served as treasurer of the youth in his church, sang in the choir, and was a model young man. One summer, after a week at camp, he came home with a trophy naming him "Mr. Youth Camp." As his interest in sports, cars, and girls blossomed, however, his submission to his religious upbringing waned. He began to slip out at night, experiment with drugs, and lie to cover up what he was doing.

When the consequences of his actions had increasingly serious effects in his young adult years, my friend turned to the Scriptures and to Christian friends for help. Still, he was unwilling or unable to yield to the God whom he needed to know personally. Having traveled widely and met people of different faiths, he questioned the worldview and belief system of his church and parents. My friend needed desperately to find his own walk with God. It seemed easier, however, time after time, to follow the path of least resistance and to do what others around him were doing with their time and energy.

Now at middle age with three children, one of whom is nearly a man himself, my friend feels trapped by his circumstances. He anxiously anticipates the problems ahead for him and his family. Meanwhile, his children follow their father's lead year by year, becoming ever more like him. My friend's inability to obey the underlying dictates of his conscience, due to circumstances of his own making, binds him and his children. The costs of disobedience and rebellion are multi-generational. They can be devastating.

The Hebrew Scriptures tell a similar saga of the lives and times of myriad personalities over hundreds of years. The bondage of sin has afflicted the human race from the beginning. Repeatedly, God has offered salvation dependent only upon obedience. Disobedience brings separation from God and divine judgment (Genesis 3:1-19; 17:1-14; Deuteronomy 5:32-33; 6:25).

Again and again, Israel and Judah fell away from following God's law and reaped disaster. The people were driven into exile or defeated in battle, the cities sacked, the women raped, the children mauled, the young men taken prisoner, and the cropland sowed with salt. In every generation a prophet arose calling the people to return to their God. Repentance, if it came, was short-lived. The nation would fall again into indolence and moral, spiritual, economic, and social decay.

Clearly, God's people could not maintain faithfulness, even for the sake of self-preservation. They seemed helpless. Their story was tragic until God's unconditional love was revealed to them through God's covenant with David.

The lectionary passages for the fourth Sunday of Advent offer good news and hope. The obedience of faith belongs to those who receive God's presence and grace and who yield themselves to God's will. Those who fulfill God's law are not the diligent legalists but the humble beneficiaries of God's mercy. When sinners experience God's unconditional love and kindness rescuing them from their self-destructive ways, their hearts are opened to adoration and willing service. Out of love for God and for fear of falling back into their old ways, they eagerly accept the guidance that will preserve them in safety (Luke 19:2-10).

When Mary, an undistinguished person encountered God, she became "the servant of the Lord" (Luke 1:38). The obedience of faith is the response of love toward the One who is gracious and present to save and to help. Out of gratitude comes upright living.

The kingdom of God is "righteousness and peace and joy in the Holy Spirit" (Romans 14:17; see also Romans 8:1-4). May God's kingdom come for my friend, for his children, and for your friends and neighbors as well. This great hope belongs, in fact, to all the world's people.

"I WILL MAKE YOU A HOUSE"
2 Samuel 7:1-11, 16

Only quiet peace and faithfulness can transform a house into a home. Yet, owning a home remains the American dream. Everybody wants a place to call their own, whether a modest bungalow or a mansion. Once that dream is realized, though, the real building must start if those who own it can expect to enjoy it.

Construction materials for the "good life" include morality and faith. The project will not get far, however, without discipline. These would build only a very modest place without forgiveness and steadfast love. In the end, a house becomes a home most fully when those who live there do so while welcoming the presence of God.

David, king of Israel, having established his capital at Jerusalem, decided to build a permanent house for himself. He built it of the best building materials imported from Lebanon. David used cedar because it was beautiful and would last. Most important, no one else could afford it. David's house was probably unique in the region and indicated his status. He was no longer a wandering warrior but a successful ruler.

Having finished that project, David conceived a second one. The other kings of the region had built not only houses for themselves but temples for their gods. David would build a permanent dwelling for his God, YHWH. If David could settle down in one place, YHWH should find rest and peace as well. David knew better than to undertake such a sacred endeavor, however, without consulting others whose business it was to know what God wanted. He reported his plan to the prophet Nathan.

At first Nathan approved and gave David God's blessing, "The LORD is with you" (2 Samuel 7:3b). It was vital to David that God go with him wherever he went to bless whatever he undertook (verse 9). This had been God's pattern from the time that David was anointed to become king over Israel.

In the night, however, Nathan had a disturbing dream that would disrupt David's plan. God spoke to the prophet and told him that God would make David a house (verse 11c). David was not to build a house for God, inasmuch as God had never asked for one nor did God need one. God wanted the freedom to move about without being identified with one place (verse 6).

Nathan delivered this surprising message to David and interpreted it in such a way that David received it as good news. God promised to make of David a dynasty and to give to him and his descendants, as well as all the people of Israel, the security of a homeland (verses 10-11a, 16). From David's lineage would come kings who would enjoy the same blessing that David had always enjoyed. God would discipline them as a father disciplines his children when they are disobedient; but God would never withdraw his love from them. God's love would be unconditional toward David and all his descendants.

David's son Solomon would build a house for God's name (2 Samuel 7:13). God, however, would not be domesticated.

The story of Nathan and David served many purposes over the course of its development and interpretation within the faith community of Israel. It authenticated the ascent of David's son to the throne rather than a man whom God appointed through a prophet. It validated the transition from a tent for the ark of the covenant to a Temple much like those of surrounding cultures.

Nathan and David's story reintroduced, for the first time since the original covenant with Abraham, the concept of a covenanting God who would keep covenant even when and if God's people broke the covenant (Genesis 12:1-3). It reassured the people of Judah in times when their kings and their nation's fortunes failed (Psalm 89). Finally, this story provided a basis for messianic hopes when the Davidic dynasty no longer ruled in Judah.

The significance of God's covenant with David becomes evident when compared with God's covenant with Moses. The Sinai covenant established a moral code given by God for the guidance of the people as they sought to move out of slavery into freedom. Obedience to God's Law would insure social cohesion and create a system of justice. God, the Lawgiver, was just and reliable. The people knew what they could expect from this God and where they stood with YHWH at all times based on an objective standard.

The Davidic covenant did not replace the law. It offered something more. It promised the people that God's presence and blessing would remain with their leaders to give them a homeland and a rest from war. It also promised discipline.

Later covenants would be needed. The Davidic covenant, however, pointed to the divine character: steadfast love and faithfulness. The Davidic covenant suggested that mercy would endure, though justice would be exercised as needed for correction.

In the context of Christian reflection, 2 Samuel 7:1-16 was understood as prophecy of the coming of Jesus, who would assume the throne of David. Jesus was the true descendant of David, born of Mary but a son of God as David had been (Psalms 2:7; 89:26-27). Jesus was the long-awaited King whose rule would be without end (Luke 1:31-33).

As the Protestant Reformation began, spiritual leaders tired of indulgences and "works righteousness" of various kinds imposed by the Roman Catholic Church. They turned to God's unconditional promise of steadfast love for David and in it found verification of their understanding of salvation by grace alone. Each generation of God's people can appropriate this story and find hope in its message.

As we reenter the text, we may choose to do so through the centerpiece of this passage, "[I] will make you a house" (2 Samuel 7:11). God has made God's faithful people a dwelling place (Romans 8:15-17; 1 Corinthians 3:16; 6:19; Ephesians 2:21). The doorway of faith remains open to us. Jesus' life, ministry, death, and resurrection make God's promised presence with us and God's steadfast love toward us plainly available.

God is with us in this house we call the church much as God remained with David. As God adopted David, making him God's son, so also we can know that we are sons and daughters of God. The sense of home we will find in this house of God, though, lies beyond the entryway or a sense of belonging. This house of God will become our home; and we will become God's home when we enter into communion with God's Spirit.

How can your church become a house worthy of God—not a status symbol or a political powerhouse but a community of people who love and obey God and who make God known by the distinctively good way in which they live?

How can God make your house a home for all who live there and for those who will visit this season?

THE MYSTERY NOW DISCLOSED
Romans 16:25-27

From childhood I have been shaped and inspired by a mountain woman whose faith shines and who is steeped in experiences of the power of God. She tells of how she grew up among churchgoing people who frequently asked her if she were a Christian. They even invited her to go to church with them. She could see nothing different about them, however, as a result of their calling themselves Christians. Their behavior and activities through the week revealed nothing of a better way of life. If she "got saved" she wanted to know it.

She did know it when it happened. As a young wife and mother, my friend gave herself and her family to the Lord, gave up the "things of this world," and moved on with God into sanctification and baptism in the Holy Spirit. She continues to experience the joy of her salvation daily and awaits being with the Lord forever with eager longing.

What attracted me to this woman when I was young was the very thing she wanted to see in her neighbors and did not. I can tell that she is different because of her faith. She knows the Lord firsthand and loves God with all her heart, soul, mind, and strength, even though her limited education and mountain seclusion restrict her understanding and her worldview. The source of her distinctiveness is the revelation she received, first through the effectual, fervent preaching of men of God and then by way of the Spirit's making the Word vivid and powerful in her soul.

Over the years, as a mainstream United Methodist Christian, I have often been recalled to my first love by her simple stories of faith and her declaration that when a person "gets saved," they will be different (Revelation 2:4). The key to a demonstration of the validity of the gospel is a changed life. It is the transformation of our entire selves that makes our witness to the Christian message winsome and the mystery plainly understood.

In a final flourish, bringing his letter to a conclusion, Paul commended his efforts "to bring about the obedience of faith" (Romans 16:26) and his witness to the non-Jewish world to the One who called him and gave him the message he proclaimed. He offered his life's work, his lengthy epistle to the saints at Rome, and his very soul to God in adoration and trust that God would be honored. Romans 16:25-27 is an act of praise to God through Jesus Christ.

Paul's goal had always been that all who believed would be made righteous through God's grace. An inner attitude of generosity, hospitality, and humility derived from the unwarranted gift of the gospel was to characterize the worldwide Christian community. The people of God were to demonstrate in their living the very will of God (12:1-2).

While Paul was praising God and entrusting his life's work to God, he continued to address the readers at Rome: "Now to God who is able to strengthen you" (16:25). His words have inspired the faith and the zeal of readers in every generation. God is the power by which humanity gains the fortitude and character through which to live well and at peace with God, self, and neighbor.

Paul believed that God's grace is eternal. It has always been at the center of God's being. God is and always has been the Giver, Sustainer, and Redeemer of life before God is the Judge and Destroyer of evil. Sadly, though, the mystery of God's forgiveness, the means of justification, and the way of obedience have been obscured, hidden by the sinful nature of humanity and the failure of the people of God to make a clear witness to God's nature.

Jesus' faith, his obedience unto death, his crucifixion, and his resurrection, however, made the hidden nature of God openly available to all, including non-Jews. As the truth about Jesus had originally been disclosed to Paul privately and directly, so now the mystery of God's grace has been openly "disclosed" through Paul's preaching and teaching of the gospel of our Lord Jesus Christ (Romans 1:17; 16:26; Galatians 1:12).

It was the faithful obedience of Jesus to the will of God in emptying himself that paved the way for those who follow him (Philippians 2:5-11). "The mystery that was kept secret for long ages" (Romans 16:25) now belongs to all who believe.

Following the life, death, and resurrection of Jesus, the Christian church, particularly those of Jewish heritage, could read the Hebrew prophets and see that many of them had anticipated the revelation that is in Jesus Christ. Paul often referred to Deuteronomy and Isaiah when interpreting the gospel (1:2; 3:21; 16:26). Paul's purpose was to demonstrate that the one who brought creation into existence, gave the law to Moses, and spoke through the prophets is the same one who further disclosed God's self in Jesus. His message was not a new doctrine of some new god but the work of "the only wise God...to whom be the glory forever" (16:27).

How are you different because of your faith in Christ?

Can others see in you an open manifestation of the truth of the gospel?

What does "the obedience of faith" mean for you at this time in your life?

MARY, MOTHER OF JESUS, DESCENDANT OF DAVID, SERVANT OF GOD
Luke 1:26-38

Mentors provide examples that we can follow. They pave the way for us by sharing their wisdom and their support with us. Christian mentors illustrate the life of faith in terms that we can understand. We can learn from watching them and model ourselves after those whose behavior and attitudes, values and lifestyle reflect what we sense to be the way of God.

Apart from role models who personify the character of true discipleship, following the Lord can feel like pioneering in strange territory alone. With a variety of these more experienced believers within our faith community, we can begin to shape our own spiritual identity and discipline.

The birth narrative of Luke's Gospel introduces the reader to several mentors in faith (Luke 1–2). Mary, the mother of Jesus, is one of these exemplars of Christian piety. Joseph, likewise, faced with a moral and spiritual challenge, proved himself faithful. Elizabeth and her husband Zechariah provide realistic models of the faith journey as well. The prophets Anna and Simeon illustrate the spirituality that should characterize the people of God.

In a critical event widely known as the Annunciation, Mary, an otherwise unknown peasant girl from Nazareth, encountered a messenger of God (Luke 1:26-38). This meeting occurred by divine initiative as an act of God. By the Word of God, coming through God's messenger, Mary was told that she would conceive and bear a child who would be King, the Son of God. Mary responded to the angel's prophecy: "Here am I, the servant of the Lord; let it be with me according to your word" (verse 38).

Had it not been for Mary's humble and submissive faith, God's initiative would have been thwarted. God's saving purpose is not forced on the unwilling. Rather, the joyous fulfillment of God's salvation comes by way of the faith and obedience of ordinary people.

Mary's most significant role in life, as in this sacred story, was to serve as a vessel of God's saving grace. This passage is not, however, ultimately about Mary or about ideal discipleship. It is about what

God has done in Jesus. The life of faithfulness is not about us and our eternal destiny but about God and God's goodness.

Let us look closely at what God has done in Jesus. First, the child to be born was to be named Jesus or "YHWH will save." Note that *Jesus* is the Greek form of the Hebrew name *Joshua*. *Joshua*, or the alternative *Jeshua*, was a common name in Palestine at the time; but its meaning, when applied to Mary's son, would be fulfilled as it had not been in any previous bearer of the name.

Second, God kept faith with the people Israel as sealed in the Davidic covenant by providing a descendant of King David who would reign in his stead (2 Samuel 7:12-16). The power of this king would never end. He would fulfill the highest expectations of the people as the "Son of the Most High," the Son of God.

The designation of Jesus as a descendant of David and an heir to his throne (Luke 1:27; 2:4; 3:23) set the stage for the later preaching of Jesus. Jesus would announce the reign of God as being at hand and "among you" (17:20-21). Jesus shunned political power and proclaimed God's reign (4:5-8; 17:20-21).

Third, Mary's son would be the Son of God. God's messenger gave the child a title that would be used frequently by the Christian church in its confession of faith and its public witness. The title designates him a divine man as well as a king. The Caesars of the Roman Empire, as well as most kings of the ancient Near East, were treated as divine appointees authorized to fulfill the work of governance by the gods. Frequently they were honored as divine representatives, if not also worshiped as gods, upon their ascension to the throne of their nation.

Frequently myths regarding their origins developed around these rulers posthumously. Luke assembled stories of Jesus' origins and events surrounding his birth in order to have the reader understand that this King, the Son of God, the Savior, was superior to all others and the completion of all previous expectations for a divinely appointed ruler. The begetting, conception, and birth of Jesus, however, were unique. Jesus was begotten by the Most High God. The conception occurred by way of the mysterious and holy action of the Divine Spirit and the obedience in faith of Mary.

People are watching your life of faith. Can they see in you the Spirit that was in Mary?

Is your most earnest desire to allow God to do with you as God wills?

Are you willing to carry about in your life span a living witness to the presence and redeeming grace of God?

What implications might surrendering your respectability and control over your destiny have?

How will you demonstrate the obedience of faith this Advent season?

Break Forth Together Into Singing

Scriptures for Christmas Day:
Isaiah 52:7-10
Hebrews 1:1-4
John 1:1-14

What would Christmas be without carols? What would worship be without hymnody and choirs? When we sing our faith, we participate in it with our entire self. We experience God with us. We pray and praise with our lips, our minds, our souls, our community of faith, and generations of saints before us.

Often the texts and tunes of the songs we sing seem appropriate only in church. Otherwise they are unreal, otherworldly, and out of touch. Rarely do the hymns we sing in worship reflect popular taste in music; yet most of us prefer it that way, for the faith we sing transcends the ordinary. It is of divine origin and inspired by the Holy Spirit.

Perhaps the dating of Jesus' birth and the celebration it calls for at the time of the Winter Solstice originated in the universal need for hope and for light at this time of year. Certainly the shortness of the winter days is not the only cause for sadness nor the only reason we need to change our mood.

Rather, the meaningless pursuit of wealth and material things with its attendant greed; pervasive injustice; intransigent disease; widespread violence, poverty, and corruption all cause us to long for something better. In this particular season, in the midst of the darkest days of the year, the mood of our singing moves out of longing and anticipation into joyous celebration. Our spirits are lifted as we sing of the coming of light and life.

SING FOR JOY
Isaiah 52:7-10

Most of us have had the experience of singing traditional Christmas music without feeling the spirit of Christmas. The songs seem dull and repetitious. The traditions feel worn and wearisome. There is no joy. We are too comfortable. We have forgotten our need of God though all is not well. We live, even in this season, as if God were absent.

Such was the condition of the exiled Judahites in Babylonia when the prophet known as Second Isaiah arose to quicken their spirits and to alert them to their great need and their great hope. His words are poetry, fitting to be sung; for they are the song of a man ecstatic in God. He stood outside of himself and his people's circumstance as he saw the return of YHWH to Zion.

Like the psalmist who composed Psalm 98, Isaiah sang with his words and with his soul. The psalmist wrote, "O sing to the LORD a new song, / for he has done marvelous things. / His right hand and his holy arm have gotten him victory" (Psalm 98:1). Isaiah's song, however, is more than a chorus of praise; it is an epic hymn.

This particular stanza of the much longer poem in which it is embedded serves as the climax or as a great crescendo. The hymn tells a story rich in imagery. Its language must not be taken literally but felt and experienced freely. It represents not a testimony of things as they are but of all that God shall cause to be.

The storyline behind the hymn includes the reality of Judah's exile in Babylonia and the concurrent destruction of Jerusalem. The walls of the Holy City are in ruins. The Temple is desolate. The people cower in humiliation under the oppression of their enemies. Both those who remain in Judah and those who live in a distant and pagan city have lost their former pride and identity. They feel that God has abandoned them. They have abandoned all hope of any return to their former glory.

God remains, however, their king. His reign has been interrupted and overthrown. Yet God will once again become their strong ruler. A new era will dawn in which YHWH will exercise sovereignty over all nations. Judah's humiliation will be transformed into peace and plenty.

YHWH, the great warrior king, will return to Zion to make his dwelling place there. From Zion, YHWH will defeat all Judah's enemies. The day of redemption is near, and the prophet has been sent to alert the people.

The image of God as king is deeply inbedded in the historical literature of the Hebrew Scriptures. Judges 8:23 portrays Gideon as being asked to rule as king. He replies, "I will not rule over you, and my son will not rule over you; the LORD will rule over you." As Samuel was considering the plea of the Hebrew people for a king, God said to Samuel, "Listen to the voice of the people in all that they say to you; for they have not rejected you, but they have rejected me from being king over them. Just as they have done to me, from the day I brought them up out of Egypt to this day, forsaking me and serving other gods, so also they are doing to you" (1 Samuel 8:7-8).

The Davidic dynasty would bring disappointment and spiritual ruin, as well as parity with the other autocracies of the region for a short period. Ultimately, however, the kings of Judah would fail; and the nation that had depended on human leaders would lose its way. Only with the return of YHWH to the throne of Judah would restoration be possible.

The author may well have been inspired to compose this great celebrative poem announcing the enthronement of YHWH after having observed the annual New Year's celebration in Babylonia in which the god Marduk was crowned with song and dance and feasting. Isaiah's celebration is of the dawning of a new age and not simply a new year. Moreover, YHWH, the living God, is to be exalted forever.

This unit of the poem can be divided into two sections or movements. The first, verses 7-8, depicts a runner returning from a battlefield with the news that the king is returning victorious. The sentinels on the wall of the city consider the runner's swift feet and joyful stride beautiful to behold. How long they have anxiously waited for any good news. This time the runner serves as an evangelist. His message is simple and sufficient: "Your God reigns" (verse 7).

YHWH no longer waited to save the people. YHWH was actively effecting the redemption of the nation. The time of salvation had arrived. The men who kept watch over Jerusalem began to sing in their joy. As they sang, the entire horizon seemed filled with the glory of the Lord. They beheld

God as if face to face, as Moses had (Numbers 14:13-14; Deuteronomy 34:10). The "glory of the LORD" was returning to Mount Zion (Isaiah 40:5).

The second section, verses 9-10, calls for a great concert of song. The songs are to be songs of victory, celebrating the power of the great warrior king who soon will bring all nations into submission (Isaiah 44:23; 49:13; 55:12). The songs that Isaiah may have had in mind include Psalms 47; 93; and 96–99, all of which express in sacred poetry the might and justice of a king. They were designed to be used in worship or at the time of a coronation ceremony or other festival. This king, of course, different from all others, would reign forever and extend his kingdom to all peoples. This king is divine and not human.

Inasmuch as we are unaccustomed to having a king and unfamiliar with thinking about our God as a warrior, how should we translate this imagery into terms that speak peace and justice for our time? Consider the words of the Advent hymn "Come, Thou Long-Expected Jesus": "Born to reign in us forever, / now thy gracious kingdom bring. / By thine own eternal spirit rule in all our hearts alone; / by thine all sufficient merit, / raise us to thy glorious throne."

The traditional Nativity pageant celebrates the Christ child. Frequently heard is the chorus of "What Child Is This": "This, this is Christ the King, / whom shepherds guard and angels sing." Hymns do what no abstract and analytical study of the terminology and theology can do. They cause us to worship, to hope, to expand the horizons of our vision so that we can see the light of truth and dare to live justly in a troubled world.

JESUS, GOD'S MOST EXCELLENT WORD
Hebrews 1:1-4

This exalted passage may well be an early hymn in praise of Christ. Scholars call it a Christological hymn. Its parallelisms, its alliteration, and its verses suggest poetry, if not hymnody. While the author wrote in the finest of Greek, many early Christians were pre-literate. They passed their faith from one to the other by word of mouth, creating an oral tradition of, for example, the sayings of Jesus.

Another means by which they preserved and celebrated their faith was through the sung liturgy of the gathered church. The earliest Christian hymns imbedded in the New Testament are glorious confessions of faith (Philippians 2:6-11; Colossians 1:15-20; 1 Timothy 3:16). These hymns articulated in majestic and yet condensed form the essential beliefs of the Christian movement. They became a part of the memory of the people.

How often have we taught Scripture to children by setting it to music. I will never forget how pleased I was to hear my son insisting that old hymns be used in Sunday school in order that the most treasured words, images, sounds, and songs of his faith might be passed down to the younger children. We can see the same intent in the author of Hebrews who borrowed from a beloved hymn in praise of Christ.

Similar hymns are used today during Advent and throughout the year. When we sing "Hail to the Lord's Anointed, / great David's greater Son," we are singing a Christological hymn. Consider also such classics as "Jesus Shall Reign," "Hope of the World," "Ye Servants of God," "Of the Father's Love Begotten," and "Christ Is the World's Light." These hymns lift us out of the realm of the visible into the heavenly domain from which our most profound hope emanates. Our hearts are stirred. Our thinking is enlightened. We stand in awe of the mystery and, in some anticipatory sense, behold him as he is.

The passage we are given as the epistle for this week's lection seeks to take a community of believers into the presence of God and of his Christ with their understanding and with their very souls. It borrows from the Wisdom tradition, including Proverbs 8:22-31, in formulating its language. Here Wisdom is personified as a woman, described as having been created before anything else, and becomes the agent of Creation. Wisdom speaks authoritatively and creatively as mediator of God's will.

God has spoken through many other means since the initial act of creation. The writer invites his readers to recall, for example, the revelation to Abram; the Flood; and Moses and all the prophets when he writes, "Long ago God spoke to our ancestors in many and various ways by the prophets" (1:1). God also spoke through plagues, visions, dreams, pillars of fire and of cloud, and by God's glory in the Temple. The reader remembers as he or she hears these words that God is one whose word is vital to the life of his people, always effectual and forever focused on their redemption.

Then the hymn shifts the reader's attention to the present, calling it "the last days." Immediately, the mood turns to one of intense anticipation. Time is short. The events at hand are critical to the course of history and the salvation of the world. God has spoken this time in the person of God's Son. Note that the author never uses the familiar name *Jesus*. The believers share a common faith. They are followers of the crucified and risen Jesus. The author is eager to lift the thinking of the reader above the historical events of the past, however, and into the realm of the reigning Lord, the one who following his resurrection has been acknowledged as God's Word.

Although previously no one recognized him or understood his eternal nature, the Son, like Wisdom, pre-existed Creation and mediated its coming into being.

The writer declares the Son to be God's heir. In using the term *heir*, the writer intends the reader to infer that the Son shares the eternal glory of God in the heavens. Consider a parallel use of the term *heir* in Paul's letter to the church at Rome: "When we cry, 'Abba! Father!' it is that very Spirit bearing witness with our spirit that we are children of God, and if children, then heirs, heirs of God and joint heirs with Christ—if, in fact, we suffer with him so that we may also be glorified with him" (Romans 8:15b-17).

With the third verse the focus of the hymn has shifted entirely to the Son. The reader is to see the Son as the image of God. In so doing, though, the vision is of the heavenly Christ rather than of the crucified one. To put it differently, the writer's appreciation for the Son in this hymn is similar to the apparition given Peter, James, and John on the Mount of Transfiguration (Mark 9:2b-3, 7). This Son does the work of the Creator God in sustaining the world. The mood evoked is awe; the appropriate response is silent adoration.

The church moved, in little more than a generation, from following a charismatic prophet of the kingdom of God in the service of the Father, Creator of heaven and earth, to worshiping the Son of God as the agent, sustainer, and redeemer of creation. What a leap of faith this represents!

The unification of the Son and the Creator that occurs in the Christology of this passage may be helpful to seekers who recognize God as Spirit present in all creation at all times. The writer's sense of mystery and awe may resonate well with the spiritual longings of a generation saturated with material things and with the scientific method.

At this point the writer introduces a theme that he will develop at some length. He portrays the Son as the great high priest who offers sacrifices for the purification of humanity, bringing to an end the Jewish sacrificial system and completing its intention for all time. The Son accomplishes the permanent forgiveness of sins for all people.

Having completed his work, the Son sits down at the right hand of God. The writer uses a circumlocution for God, just as he has avoided the name of Jesus, referring to God by the title "Majesty" (Hebrews 1:3). Clearly the human-like image of the heavenly Son sitting is symbolic. It signifies the power given the Son by God to rule. He has taken up divine authority in the heavenly realm, second only to God, and shall act on God's behalf. The writer is eager to assert that the Son is superior in all ways to any other heavenly being, especially the angels (verse 4). All in heaven and on earth must submit to the Son.

Note that the writer was a Jewish Christian and wrote to Jewish Christians. For this reason he used images familiar to them from their apocalyptic and wisdom literature,

as well as from their traditional worship. He used beliefs that were embraced by what became the dominant Jewish religious party in the first century (the Pharisees), including angels existing in a heavenly realm that paralleled the historical domain and where God held court with many servants and subjects.

Like the Pharisees, the writer honored the Jewish sacrificial system by showing how Jesus fulfilled it. The contemporary student of the Book of Hebrews, interested in learning from the writer's work, can recognize the value of communicating the faith in the religious vernacular of one's audience. The writer was effective as a preacher and teacher because of his agility with language, both in the structure and design of his composition and in his creative use of symbolic meaning. In every culture such creative genius, when melded with Christian vision, can communicate the faith in an empowering and transformational way.

What hymn, spiritual song, or other creative act of worship might the Word of God inspire in your heart this season?

THE WORD OF GOD MADE FLESH
John 1:1-14

The prologue to John's Gospel has hymn-like qualities. Many scholars have discovered in its lines what appears to be remnants of a hymn that predated the Gospel of John. Anyone who reads this introduction senses its lofty vision, its exalted understanding of the creative Word incarnate, and its power as a vehicle of worship.

The prologue introduces themes such as life and light that the writer will develop further in the body of his Gospel. At the same time, it uses terms such as *logos* and *grace* never repeated in the rest of the Gospel, making the vocabulary seem foreign to the usual style of the writer. This suggests that the writer borrowed a liturgical confession of faith or hymn from an earlier tradition in order to introduce his message in the most moving and exalted style available.

This hymn-like prologue has three or four movements, each building on the previous movement toward a climax. The first movement features the word images of life and light (verses 1-5). The second movement, possibly an insertion, features John the Baptist as a witness to the Light. The third movement, found in verses 9-13, depicts the true light coming into the world in order to give birth to children of God. The final verse provides the climax of the hymn: "And the Word became flesh and lived among us, and we have seen his glory, the glory as of a father's only son, full of grace and truth" (verse 14).

Some scholars have explored the possibility that the prologue to John's Gospel introduces concepts and vocabulary native to Greek philosophy and religion rather than to the Jewish faith or to the message and teaching of Jesus. While the writer of the Gospel of John thought and wrote in a Greco-Roman cultural context, he was, nevertheless, a Jewish Christian writing to Jewish Christians.

The Roman Empire controlled the political and economic lives of the Jewish people in this period. Its culture, primarily Hellenistic, was pervasive. Its literature, both mythology and philosophy, was widely read by the educated class of whom the writer of John's Gospel was surely a member. Nonetheless, a careful reading of the Gospel as a whole, as well as the prologue, will demonstrate the Jewish foundations of the evangelist's faith and message.

Basic to this hymn is the Greek word *logos*, translated into English as *word*. Notice that it is used as a title throughout the prologue. It refers to Jesus as the creative will of God ordering Creation and overcoming chaos first introduced in Genesis 1:1-3.

Parallel uses of the term can be found outside the New Testament. In Stoic writing of the same period, the term *logos* is used as a reference to the rational order of the universe, a philosophical category rather than a personal divinity. Philo, a Jewish philosopher, teacher, and writer of the late first century, used the term to refer to the creative plan of God that governs the world. Here the writer uses it to establish his Christology or his thinking about the identity of Jesus as continuous with the God who spoke creation into being as described in Genesis 1:1 and the same as God: "The Word was God" (John 1:1). Notice, however, the hymn's symbolic use of the terms *life* and *light,* paralleling but not replicating the original Creation story.

Some have argued that the hymn was composed as a response to pre-Gnostic materials. Some propose that it was taken from an early liturgy developed within an unorthodox Christian community dominated by Greek or Egyptian thought and influenced by mystery cults spread throughout the Mediterranean basin. Gnostics of the second century denied the humanity and death of Jesus, saw as the goal of faith the transcendence of physical existence that it viewed as entirely negative, and believed that one must have secret knowledge of God in order to enter into life and light.

This hymn announces the physical humanity of Jesus (verse 14) and in so doing pronounces life in the flesh good. Moreover, it proclaims that the life and light that the Word brings is universally available to all who believe, requiring no elitist rituals of initiation or esoteric indoctrination.

Behind the hymn-like prologue to the Gospel of John is a worldview peculiar to John's faith community and distinctive among the canonical Christian literature. In some ways it seems more like that of the Gospel of Thomas, a Gnostic gospel, than those of Mark, Matthew, or Luke. Nonetheless it is not discontinuous with the widespread apocalyptic vision of the period.

The writer believed the universe to be divided into two realms: the visible and the invisible, the eternal and the temporal. Moreover, he believed that a contest was underway during the time of Jesus between good and evil or light and darkness. He assumed that an ultimate conflict between these two spheres of influence must occur. The Word would necessarily play the critical role. That conflict reached its resolution in the crucifixion of Jesus, the moment of his greatest triumph and glorification (Philippians 2:1-11).

The defeat of Satan, death, and darkness began in Jesus' obedience unto death and in his resurrection. They will never again control the fate of those who believe. Through faith in Jesus, then, the believer participates in Jesus' triumph and enters into life eternal.

May the light of Christ, the coming King, illumine your heart and mind as you sing your faith this Christmastide.